Cat's Cradle, Owl's Eyes: A Book of
String Games

ᗊᗊᗊᗊᗊᗊᗊᗊᗊᗊᗊᗊᗊᗊᗊᗊᗊᗊᗊᗊᗊ

by Camilla Gryski

Illustrated by Tom Sankey

William Morrow and Company
New York | 1984

Text copyright © 1983 by Camilla Gryski
Illustrations copyright © 1983 by Tom Sankey
Cover photograph copyright © 1983 by Mark Zelinski

First published in Canada in 1983 by Kids Can Press, Toronto, Ontario.

Library of Congress Cataloging in Publication Data
Gryski, Camilla.   Cat's cradle, owl's eyes: a book of string games.
Summary: Presents basic information for making string figures and gives step-by-step instructions for more than twenty specific figures. 1. String figures—Juvenile literature. [1. String figures. 2. Games] I. Sankey, Tom, ill. II. Title. GV1218.S8G78 1984   793'.9   84-9075
ISBN 0-688-03940-5 (lib. bdg.)
ISBN 0-688-03941-3 (pbk.)

To Mark and Damian and all the children at the Hospital for Sick Children

My thanks to Ken McCuaig and Bill Russell who started it all, to my father, Denis Milton who took hundreds of photographs of my hands, and to my family who played cat's cradles with me, often late into the night.

Contents

Introduction

Cat's cradles, or string figures, are designs you weave on your fingers with a loop of string.

We don't know when people first started playing with string, or which primitive people invented this ancient art. We do know that all primitive societies had and used string—for hunting, fishing, and weaving—and that string figures have been collected from native peoples all over the world.

The Inuit, for example, create some of the most complicated and beautiful string figures ever recorded. And because string figures are known throughout the world, from south-east Asia and Japan to South America and the West Indies, they continue to come to Canada with newcomers from many lands.

Making string figures was a pastime and an art. The string artist was often a storyteller as well, using his loop of string to illustrate his tale. The string figures were of animals or stars or other things from nature. Some figures moved and some were like magic.

As you do the string figures in this book, you will learn a little about the people who did them many years ago: what they used for string, what superstitions they had about playing string games, what things were important to them, and what things made them laugh.

It is best to start with the easier figures at the beginning of the book, and when you feel comfortable with the string on your fingers, go on to those figures that have more steps and are more complicated.

At first you will have to remember all the steps it takes to make a figure, but very soon your fingers will remember for you. And the more figures you do, the easier it will be to understand the language that tells you and your fingers what to do next.

So learn these figures—and share them with your friends. Maybe they can show you some new ones. You can experiment too; you may invent something wonderful.

And remember: always carry a string in your pocket!

Anthropologists used to be described as people with their pockets full of string.

About the String

The Inuit used sinew or a leather thong to make their string figures. Other peoples further south made twine from the inside of bark. We are told that Tikopian children in the Pacific Islands area preferred fibre from the hibiscus tree, although they would use a length of fishing line if it was handy. Some people even used human hair, finely braided.

Fortunately, you don't have to go out into the woods or cut your hair to get a good string for making string figures.

You can use ordinary white butcher's string knotted together at the ends. Macrame cord also works quite well, as it is thicker than string. A thicker string loop will better show off your string figures.

Dressmaker's supply stores sell nylon cord (usually by the metre). This kind of cord is probably the best, and because it is woven, not plied or twisted, it won't crease. It can be joined without a knot. A knot in your string loop can cause tangles, and figures that move won't go smoothly if there is a knot in the way.

How to Make Your String

You need about two metres of string or cord, so that your string loop will measure one metre when it is joined. This is a standard size. If this length seems uncomfortably long, a shorter string is fine for most of the figures.

The string can be either tied or melted together.

To tie your string

You need a knot that won't slip, so a square knot is best.

1. Lay the right end of the string across the left end.

2. Put this right end under the left string to tie the first part of the knot.

3. Lay the new left end across the new right end.

4. Put this new left end under the new right string and tighten the knot.

5. Trim the ends to make the knot neat.

To melt your string

If the cord is nylon or some other synthetic fibre, you can melt the ends together. Joining the string takes practice, and it has to be done quickly while the cord is hot. You will probably need some help, so please do this with an adult.

1. Hold the ends of the string near each other, about one to two centimetres above a candle flame. If the ends are not melting at all, they are too far away from the flame. They will singe if you are holding them too close.

2. When the ends are gooey, stick them together.

3. Count to five to let them cool, then roll them between your fingers to smooth the joint.

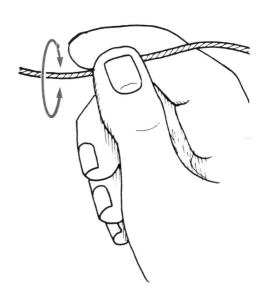

You have now made your "play string" or "ayahaak" as the Inuit call it.

Terminology
There's a Special Language

A long time ago, people made lists of the names of string figures, or brought back drawings of the finished patterns. Some even kept the string pattern itself, fastened to a piece of paper.

But once a string figure is finished, it is almost impossible to tell just how it was made. We can learn and teach each other string figures today because, in 1898, two anthropologists, Dr. A.C. Haddon and Dr. W.H.R. Rivers, invented a special language to describe the way string figures are made. Haddon and Rivers developed their special language to record all the steps it took to make the string figures they learned in the Torres Straits. Then, other anthropologists used this same language, or a simpler version of it, when they wanted to remember the string figures they saw in their travels.

The language used in this book to describe the making of the figures is similar to that used by Haddon and Rivers. The loops and the strings have names, and there are also names for some of the basic positions and moves.

About Loops

When the string goes around your finger or thumb, it makes a **loop**.

The loops take their names from their location on your hands: **thumb loop**, **index loop**, **middle finger loop**, **ring finger loop**, **little finger loop**.

If you move a loop from one finger to another, it gets a new name: a loop that was on your thumb but is now on your little finger is a new little finger loop.

Each loop has a **near string**—the one nearer (or closer) to you—and a **far string**—the one farther from you.

If there are two loops on your thumb or finger, one is the **lower loop**—the one near the base of your thumb or finger—and the other is the **upper loop**—the one near the top of your thumb or finger. Don't get these loops mixed up, and be sure to keep them apart.

About Making the Figures

As you make the figures in this book, you will be weaving the strings of the loops on your fingers. Your fingers or thumbs can go over or under the strings to pick up one or more strings, then go back to the basic position.

Sometimes you may **drop** or **release** a loop from your fingers.

It takes a little while to get used to holding your hands so that the strings don't drop off your fingers. If you accidentally drop a loop or a string, it is best to start all over again.

Now go and get your string—let's begin!

Names of the Strings

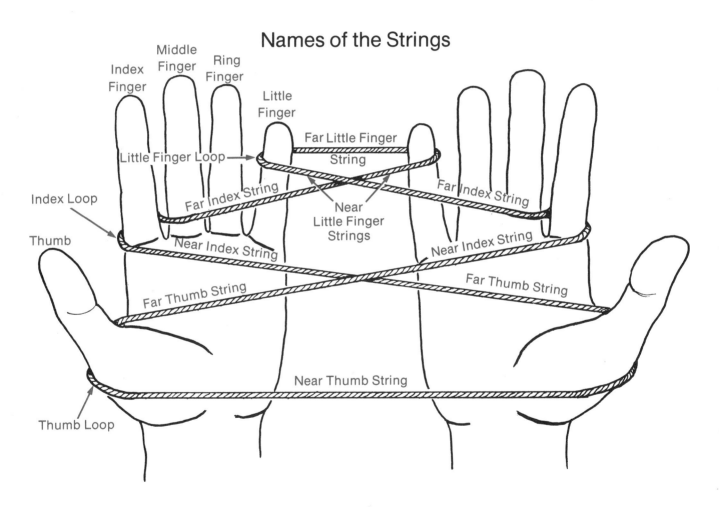

The Basic Position

Your hands begin in the **basic position** for most string figures and usually return to the basic position after each move.

1. Your hands are parallel, the palms are facing each other, and your fingers are pointing up.

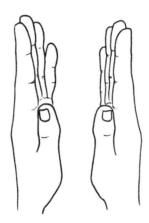

The hands in some of the pictures are not in the basic position. The hands are shown with the palms facing you so that you can see all the strings clearly.

Position 1

1. With your hands in the basic position, hang the loop of string on your thumbs. Stretch your hands as far apart as you can, to make the string loop tight.

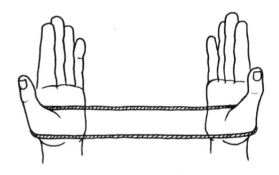

2. Pick up the far thumb string with your little fingers. The string that goes across the palm of your hand is called the **palmar string**.

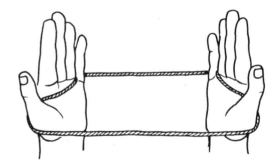

Opening A

Many string figures begin with **Opening A**.

1. Put the string loop on your fingers in Position 1.

2. With your right index finger, pick up from below the palmar string on your left hand, and return to the basic position pulling this string on the back of your index finger as far as it will go.

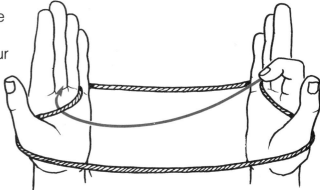

3. With your left index finger, pick up the right palmar string, from below, in between the strings of the loop that goes around your right index finger. Return to the basic position, again pulling out the palmar string as far as it will go.

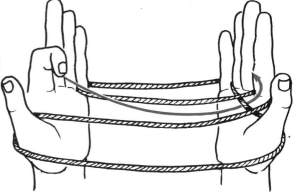

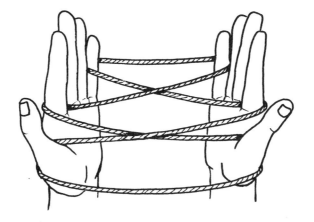

To Navaho a Loop

When you have two loops on your thumb or finger, a lower loop and an upper loop, you **Navaho** these loops by lifting the lower loop—with the thumb and index finger of your opposite hand, or with your teeth—up over the upper loop and over the tip of your finger or thumb.

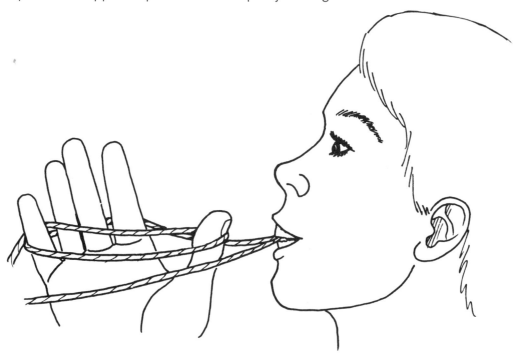

You can also Navaho a loop by tipping down your thumb or finger, letting the lower loop slip off, then straightening up your thumb or finger again.

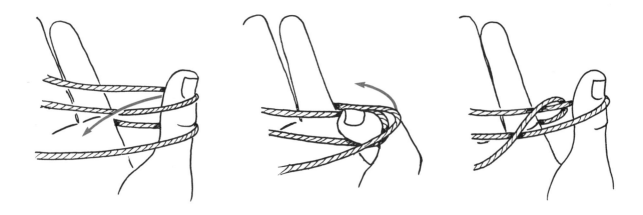

To Share a Loop

Sometimes you will **share a loop** between two fingers or a finger and your thumb. You use your opposite index finger and thumb to pull out the loop so that the other finger or thumb will fit into the loop as well.

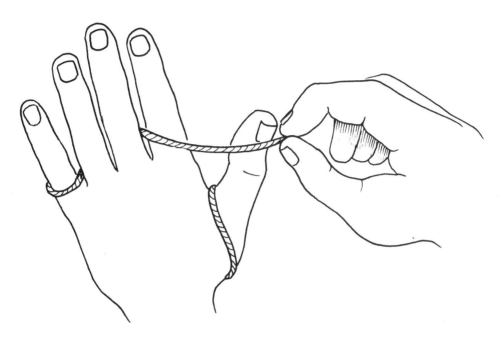

To Extend a Figure

Sometimes the strings may be woven and a figure may be finished, but it needs to be **extended** by pulling the hands apart, or by turning or twisting the hands in a certain way. Extending the figure makes a tangle of strings magically turn into a beautiful pattern.

To Take the Figure Apart

Always take the figures apart gently, as tugging creates knots. If the figure has top and bottom straight strings which frame the pattern, pull these apart and the pattern will dissolve.

Getting a String or Strings

When the instructions tell you to **get** a string or strings, your finger or thumb goes under that string, picks up that string on its back (the back of your finger or thumb is the side with the fingernail); then returns to the basic position carrying the string with it. The instructions will tell you if you are to use your fingers or thumb to pick up the strings in a different way.

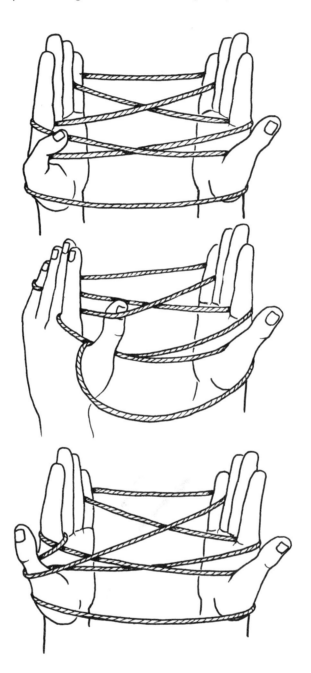

How to Double a String

For some figures, you can use a short string loop, or you can double your long string.

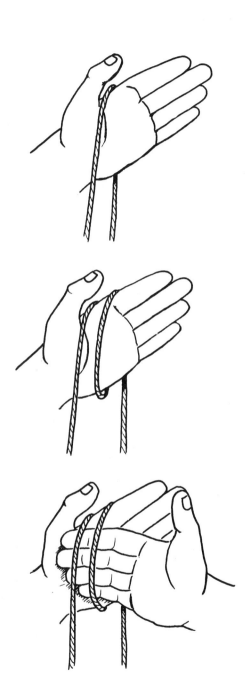

1. Hang the string loop over the fingers but not the thumb of your hand.

2. Wrap the back string of the hanging loop once around your hand.

3. Take hold of everything that crosses the palm of your hand (the loop and one hanging string) and pull these strings out as far as they will go.

Cup and Saucer

We call this figure a Cup and Saucer, but originally it came from New Caledonia where it represented a canoe with an outrigger attached to one side. In Japan, it is called a house when it is upside down, and a saki cup when right side up!

Double your long string (see page 17 for instructions) or use a short string loop for this figure.

1. Do Opening A.

2. Your thumbs go over the far thumb strings, over the near index strings, then under the far index strings to get them and bring them towards you. Return your thumbs to the basic position. Each thumb now has two loops.

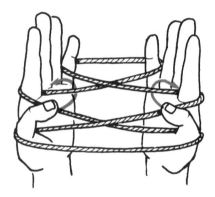

3. Navaho the loops on your left thumb. Now Navaho the loops on your right thumb. (See page 14 for instructions on how to Navaho a loop.)

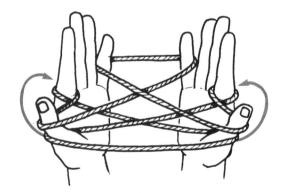

4. Your little fingers drop their loops.

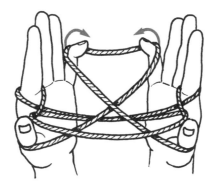

5. Your thumbs pull out their loops to extend the Cup and Saucer.

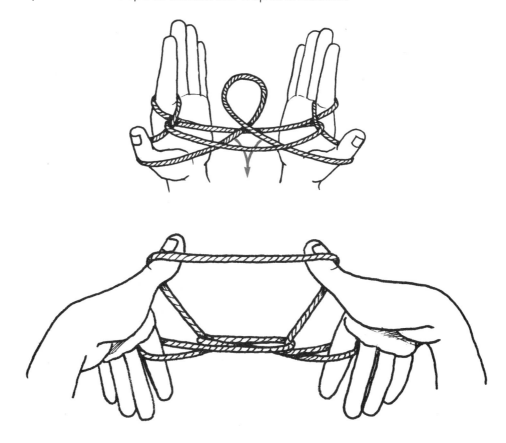

Don't drop this figure if you want to go on to Owl's Eyes on the next page.

Owl's Eyes

Owl's Eyes is a continuation of the Cup and Saucer. When you've completed the figure, put the Owl's Eyes up to your own eyes and make owl sounds.

1. Make the Cup and Saucer.

2. Your thumbs go from underneath up into the index loops (up into the saucer).
    *Now you have two loops on each thumb.

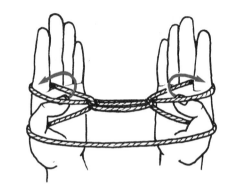

3. Navaho the thumb loops.

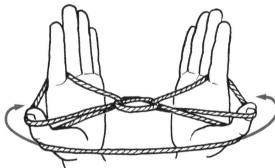

4. Your index fingers hook over the long string which crosses the middle of the figure, and down into the index loops.

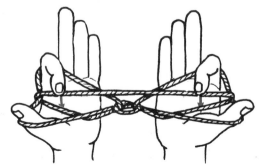

5. Turn your hands so that the palms face away from you. Don't worry about the index loops. They will just slip off your index fingers.

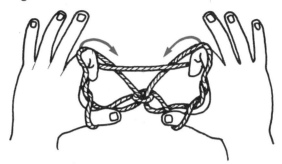

6. Your index fingers straighten up to extend Owl's Eyes.

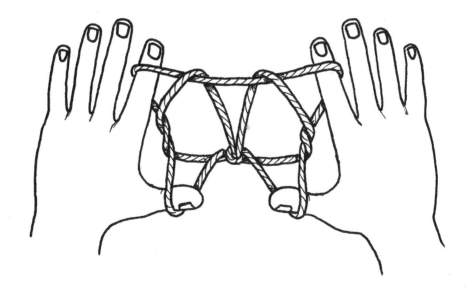

Some Inuit would not play cat's cradles in the sunshine. A legend said that the sun once saw a man playing cat's cradles and tickled him.

The Fish Spear

This string figure represented a fish spear or harpoon to the people who lived in the Torres Straits between Australia and New Guinea, a duck spear in Alaska, and a coconut palm tree in Africa. The Salish Indians call it Pitching a Tent. You can call it a witch's broom, especially at Hallowe'en!

1. Do Position 1.

2. Your right index finger goes under the left palmar string and pulls it out a little bit.

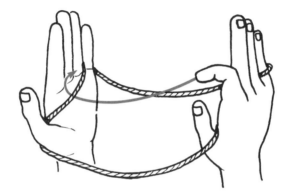

3. Your right index finger **twists its loop**. (See instructions below on How to Twist a Loop.)

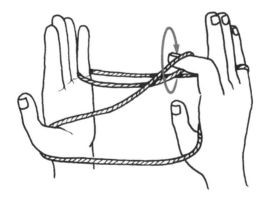

> **How to Twist a Loop**
> Rotate your index finger away from you, down, towards you and up. Make sure the twist is in the string loop, not around your index finger.

Do it again. *There are now two twists in the strings of the right index loop.

4. Your right index finger pulls out its twisted loop as far as it will go.

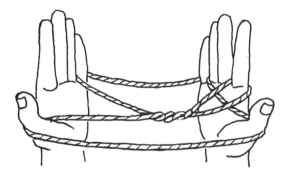

5. Your left index finger picks up, from below, the right palmar string between the strings of the right index loop. Now pull this loop out as far as it will go.

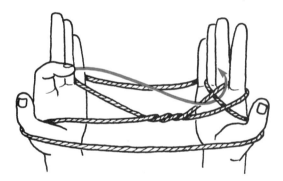

6. Your right thumb and right little finger drop their loops. Pull your right index finger out as far as it will go so that the loops move up the string towards your left hand. Now you've made the Fish Spear.

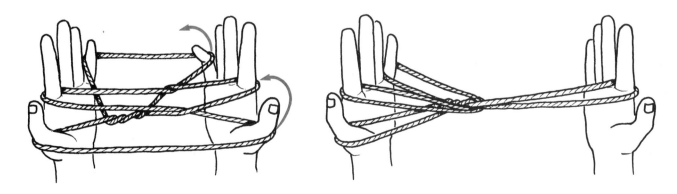

The Winking Eye

This string figure came from the Hawaiian island of Kauai. Use your imagination and you can really see the eye wink.

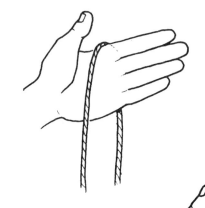

1. Hang the string loop over the fingers (but not the thumb) of your left hand.

2. Your left middle, ring and little fingers close on the string hanging down across the palm of your hand. Your index finger still points out.

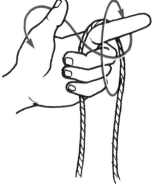

3. Your right index finger and thumb take the back string of the hanging loop, wrap it all the way around your left index finger, then bring it forward to hang up on your thumb.

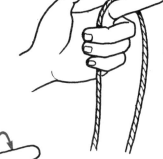

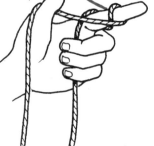

4. Your right index finger and thumb pull out the loop around your left index finger to share it with your left thumb. Be careful not to twist the loop when you do this.

5. Take the string of the hanging loop which is nearest to you, lift it up over the string which runs between your index finger and thumb, and let it hang down in front of this string between your index finger and thumb.

6. Take the other string of the hanging loop (the one you have been holding) and lift it up to hang over your thumb.

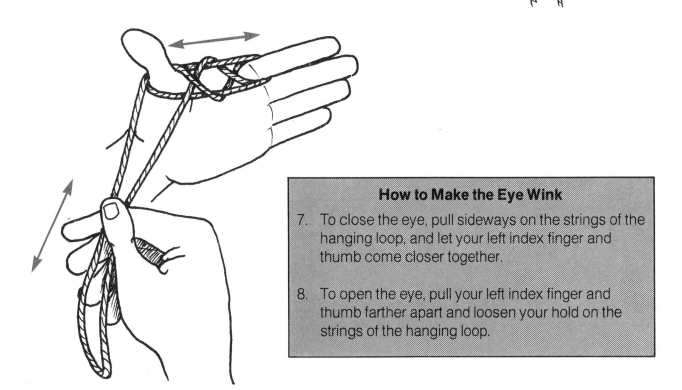

How to Make the Eye Wink

7. To close the eye, pull sideways on the strings of the hanging loop, and let your left index finger and thumb come closer together.

8. To open the eye, pull your left index finger and thumb farther apart and loosen your hold on the strings of the hanging loop.

The Parachute and the Bunch of Keys

This old-fashioned parachute from Scotland turns into a bunch of keys. The figure has a lot of steps, but don't let that discourage you. It's not as hard as it looks.

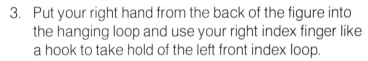

1. Do Position 1 on your left hand.

2. Put the palmar string behind your middle finger.

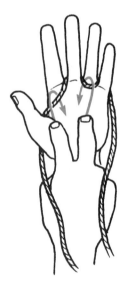

3. Put your right hand from the back of the figure into the hanging loop and use your right index finger like a hook to take hold of the left front index loop.

   Use your right middle finger like a hook to take hold of the front ring finger loop.

   Pull these loops out as far as they will go, letting the long string loop slide off your wrist.

   *Your right index finger and right middle finger are each holding a loop. There is a space between the loops.

4. Your left index finger goes down into the loop held by your right index finger.

   Your left middle finger goes down into the space between the loops.

   Your left ring finger goes down into the loop held by your right middle finger.

5. Hang these loops over the back of your left hand and let go of the strings.

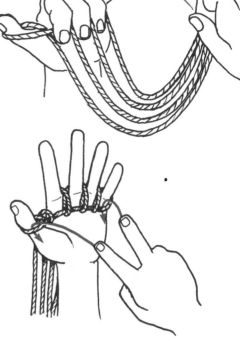

6. Use your right index finger like a hook to take hold of the left front thumb loop.

   Use your right middle finger like a hook to take hold of the left front little finger loop.

7. Pull out these loops carefully to make the Parachute.

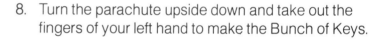

8. Turn the parachute upside down and take out the fingers of your left hand to make the Bunch of Keys.

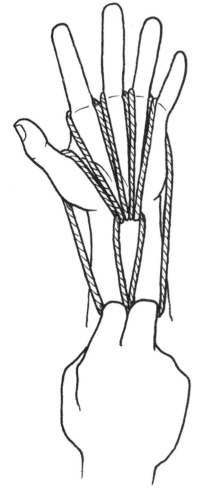

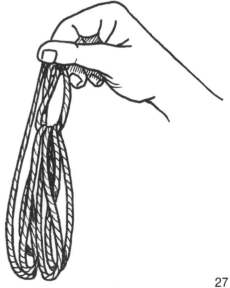

Cutting the Hand

To trick and trap your friends, try this Inuit figure. One minute your friend's wrist is caught in a tangle of strings, the next—it's free!

1. Do Opening A.

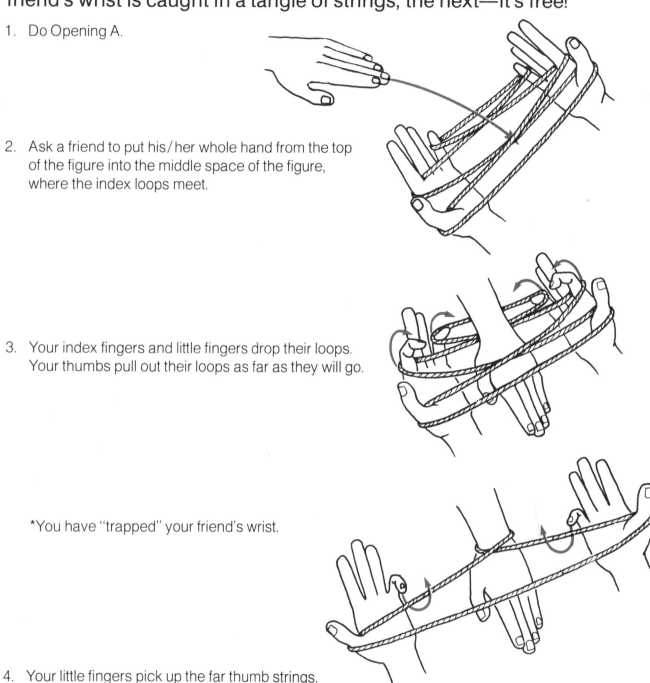

2. Ask a friend to put his/her whole hand from the top of the figure into the middle space of the figure, where the index loops meet.

3. Your index fingers and little fingers drop their loops. Your thumbs pull out their loops as far as they will go.

   *You have "trapped" your friend's wrist.

4. Your little fingers pick up the far thumb strings.

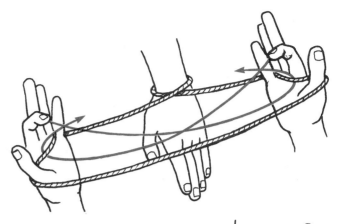

5. Do Opening A again. Don't let your friend out of the trap yet.

6. Ask your friend to put his/her hand back up through the middle space where the index loops meet, but from the bottom of the figure this time.

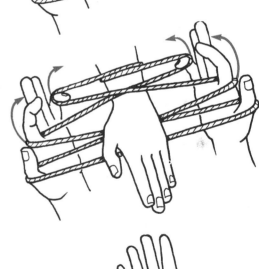

7. Your index fingers and little fingers drop their loops again. When your thumbs pull out their loops this time, your friend's hand will magically be free.

The Siberian House

This Inuit figure is a little more difficult than the others you've been doing, but it's worth the effort. Hold on to the house once you've made it, because the next step shows the house breaking, and the two people running away in opposite directions.

1. Do Opening A.

2. Turn your hands so that your palms are facing you, and put all your fingers down into the thumb loops.

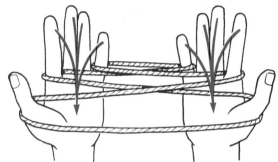

3. Throw the thumb loops over the backs of your hands and return your hands to the basic position. Be sure to keep all the loops separate. The loops around the backs of your hands should be lower than the index loops.

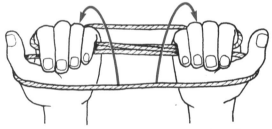

4. Your thumbs hook down the strings that go around the backs of your hands (the near strings of the hand loops), and go under all the other strings to pick up, from below, the far string of the hand loop. Return under the strings of the index loops. You now have a loop on each thumb.

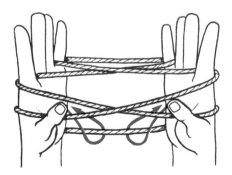
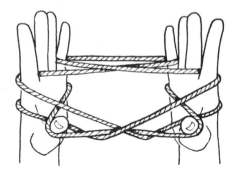

5. With your right thumb and index finger, take hold of the string that goes around the back of your left hand and lift it up over your fingers (but not over your thumb), to lie on the palm side of your left hand.

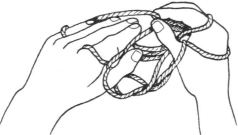

*Be careful not to lose any of the loops on your right fingers as you do this.

6. With your left thumb and index finger, take hold of the string that goes around the back of your right hand and lift it up over your fingers (but not your thumb) to lie on the palm side of your right hand.

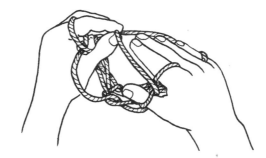

This is the Siberian House.

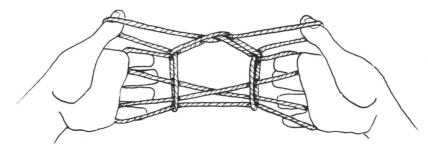

7. When you release the loops from your index fingers and pull out gently with your hands, you can see two people running away in opposite directions.

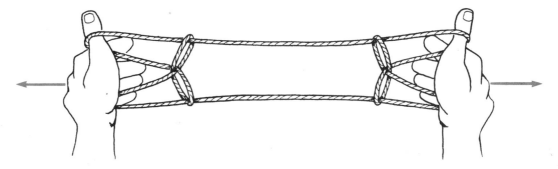

Cheating the Hangman

This is another string trick that works like magic. It was collected from the Philippines and is also found in Japan. Please be careful with this one.

1. Hang the string loop around your neck.

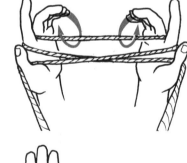

2. With your right hand, take hold of the right string of the loop and gently wrap it once around your neck.

3. Make Position 1, then Opening A with the strings of the hanging loop.

4. Your little fingers drop their loops. Pull your hands apart as far as they will go.

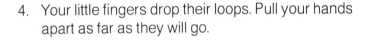

5. Your middle, ring and little fingers go up into the index loops. Now all your fingers are in the index loops.

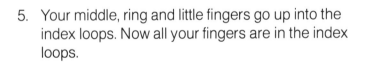

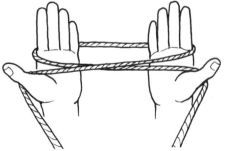

6. Your index, middle, ring and little fingers close down on the far thumb and near index strings.

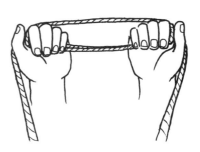

7. Your fingers are holding on to a string loop which has one string at the top and two strings at the bottom. Turn this string loop upside down so that there are two strings at the top and one string at the bottom.

8. Now put your head, chin first, right through the loop held by your hands. The loop is now hanging around your neck.

9. When you let go of the string loop, one long string loop will hang down the front. With your hands, gently pull out the sides of this loop and the string will come free.

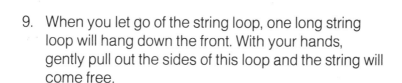

If the string loop doesn't come free, make sure it isn't just tangled in your collar or your hair.

The Hogan and the Bunch of Bananas

This figure represents a Navaho tent, which is called a Hogan. It also makes a bunch of bananas. Are you hungry?

1. Hang the string loop around the back of the index and middle fingers of your left hand. The long loop hangs down across your palm.

2. Your right index finger goes into the hanging loop from behind, then between your left index and middle finger. Use this finger like a hook to take hold of the string that goes behind your left index and middle fingers.

   Pull this loop out as far as it will go, letting the string loop slide off your wrist. Let go of the string.

3. Your right hand goes into the long hanging loop from below. Your right thumb and index finger take hold of the strings which go between your left index and middle finger. Make sure that you pick them up above the single front loop.

4. Pull out these strings as far as they will go, letting the wrist loop slide off your right hand as you pull. Keep holding the loop with your right thumb and index finger. Be careful not to twist the loop.

   Now make this loop wider by putting the rest of the fingers of your right hand into the loop.

   *This double string loop has two top strings (the strings that run between your left index and middle finger), and two bottom strings.

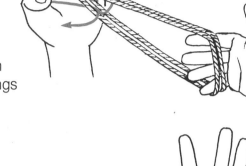

5. Your left thumb and little finger each take, from below, one of the bottom strings. Drop the strings held by your right hand.

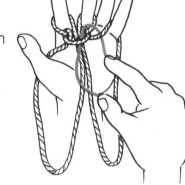

6. There is a small loop that goes around the loops on your left index and middle fingers. With your right thumb and index finger, gently pull out this small loop. Don't pull too far or the figure will fall apart.

7. This is the Navaho Hogan.

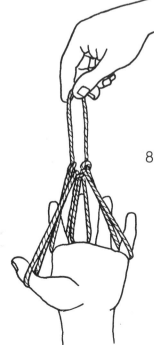

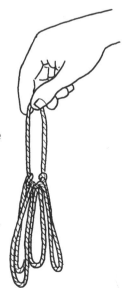

8. When you take the fingers of your left hand out of their loops, you have the Bunch of Bananas. See if your friends can pick one banana without taking the whole bunch.

The Saw

This figure of the saw is found in many parts of the world. This is the way people in Scotland made it. As they sawed, they chanted:

See saw, Johnnie Maw,
See san, Johnnie Man.

1. Put the string loop behind the index, middle, and ring fingers of each hand.

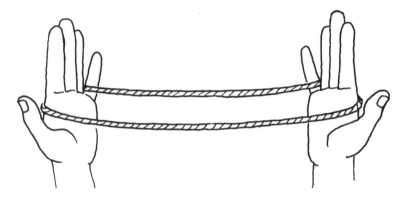

2. With the index finger and thumb of your right hand, take the near string of the loop around the fingers of your left hand and wrap it once around your left index, middle, and ring fingers.

3. With the index finger and thumb of your left hand, take the near string of the loop around the fingers of your right hand and wrap it once around the index, middle, and ring fingers of your right hand.

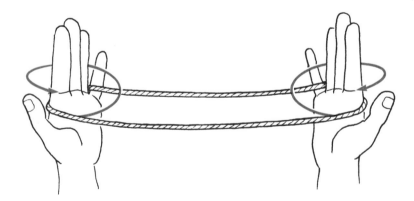

4. Now complete as in Opening A using your middle fingers.

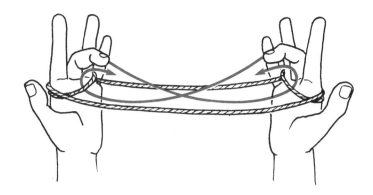

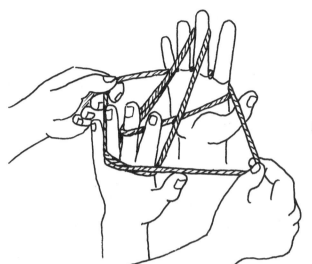

5. Ask a friend to take hold of the long strings that run from one hand to the other at the bottom of the figure.

6. Press the index, middle, and ring fingers of each hand tightly together so that the middle finger loops don't slip off. Then take your hands out of the figure. Now, the only loops on your hands are around your middle fingers. Tell your friend to hang on to his/her strings. You and your friend can now easily slide the strings back and forth like a saw and chant the verse.

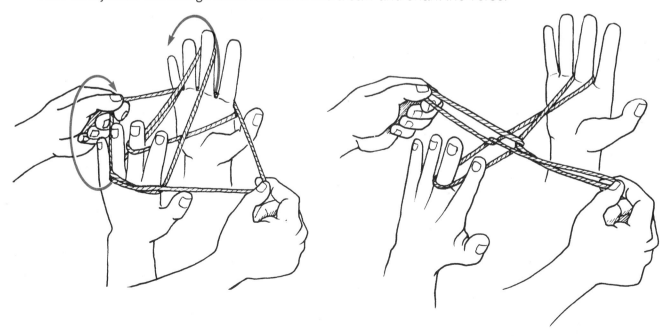

The Twitcher

This string figure originally came from the South Pacific. In some places, it was called Mrs. Crab. You'll have to use your imagination to see Mrs. Crab walking along. In Hawaii it was called the Twitcher, but when it travelled to Japan, it became known as the Elastic Band.

Double your long string or use a short loop for this figure.

1. Do Position 1.

2. Your fingers are pointing up. Point them away from you. Now your thumbs are pointing up and the string loop has a top string and a bottom string.

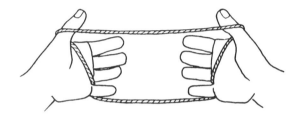

3. Slide your hands along the string loop until your thumbs touch the bottom string. Now your thumbs are pointing down. Move your fingers sideways towards each other until your hands look exactly like the ones in the picture.

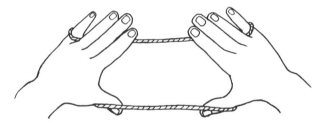

4. Catch the bottom string on the backs of your thumbs and return your hands to the basic position. Now your fingers are pointing up and there are loops on your thumbs and little fingers.

5. Your thumbs get the near little finger string and return.

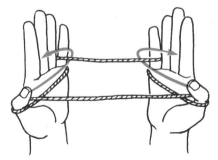

6. Your little fingers get the far thumb string and return.

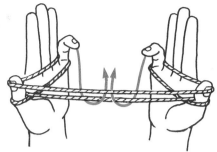

7. From above, put your index fingers down into the loops between your little fingers and thumbs, and on their backs, pick up the front palmar strings.

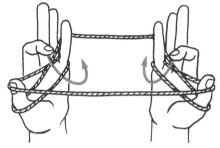

8. Tip your thumbs down (or use your mouth), to let the upper straight thumb string slide off your thumbs.

9. Tip your little fingers down (or use your mouth), to let the upper straight little finger string slide off your little fingers.

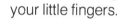

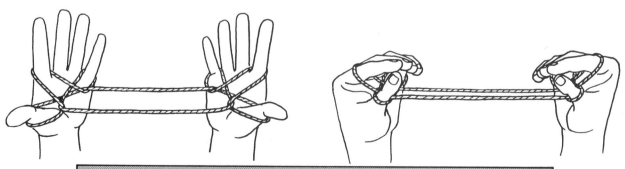

How to make the Twitcher twitch or the Elastic Band stretch

10. Stretch your fingers apart and your hands will move close together.
11. Now let your fingers collapse and pull your hands apart.

The Fishnet

The figure of the Fishnet appeared in many parts of the world. The Osage Indians called it Osage Diamonds. Among other tribes, it was known as Jacob's Ladder. In Africa, it was called a Calabash Net—a net used for carrying a large gourd. And in Quebec, it's Le pont de Québec, the Quebec Bridge.

1. Do Opening A.

2. Your thumbs drop their loops.

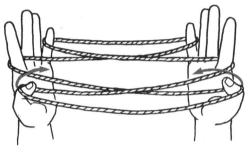

3. Turn your hands away from you with the palms facing out and the thumbs facing down.

4. Your thumbs pick up from below the far little finger string (the bottom string), and return under the strings of the index loops.

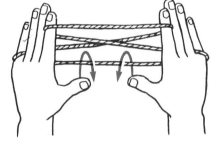

5. Your thumbs go over the near index string to get the far index strings and return.

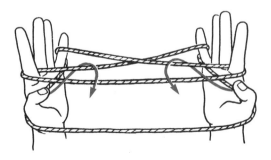

6. Your little fingers drop their loops.

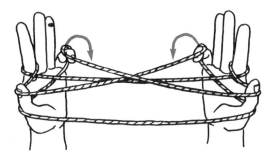

7. Your little fingers go over the near index strings to get the far thumb strings and return.

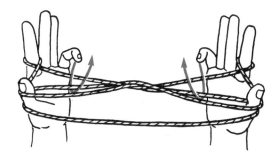

8. Your thumbs drop their loops. This is **Cat's Whiskers**. You can meow if you like!

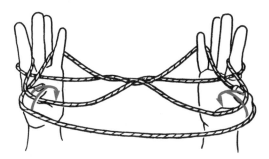

9. Your thumbs go over both strings of the index loops to get the near little finger strings and return.

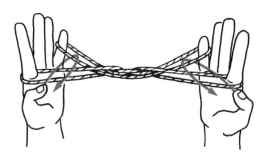

Keep going ...

10. Use your right thumb and index finger to pull out the left index loop and share it with your left thumb.

11. Do this again to share the right index loop with your right thumb.

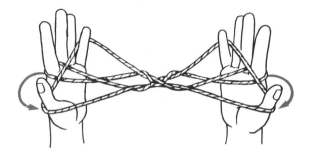

12. Tip your thumbs down (or use your fingers or teeth), to Navaho first the left thumb loops, then the right.

13. Near each thumb there is a string triangle. Your index fingers go down into these triangles.

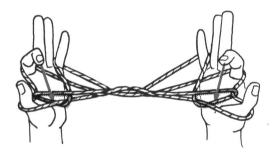

14. Gently take your little fingers out of their loops.

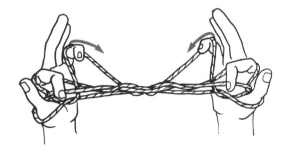

15. Turn your hands so that the palms face away from you. Don't worry about the index loops. They will just slip off your index fingers.

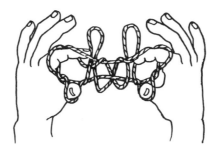

16. Your index fingers straighten up to extend the Fishnet.

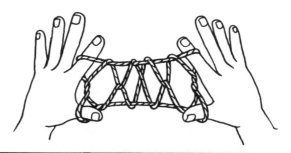

To avoid squashed diamonds
Don't pull your hands apart; just stretch your index fingers and thumbs as you extend the net.

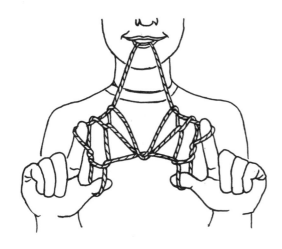

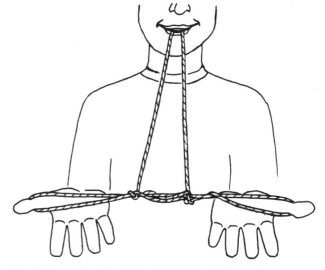

17. To make the **Eiffel Tower**, with your teeth, pick up the top string of the net between the two middle diamonds and pull. Keep hanging on to that string with your teeth. Now you can go on to make the Witch's Hat.

18. To make the **Witch's Hat**, pick up the top string of the net between the two middle diamonds. Your index fingers drop their loops and you pull down with your thumbs.

Man Climbing a Tree

Someone looked at a drawing of this completed figure and worked backwards through all the steps to recreate the man climbing the tree. This is one string puzzle that was solved! Man Climbing a Tree is originally from Australia. You will see that the higher the man climbs, the smaller he gets.

1. Do Opening A.

2. Turn your hands so that your palms are facing you.

3. Your little fingers go over all the strings to get the near thumb string and then return.

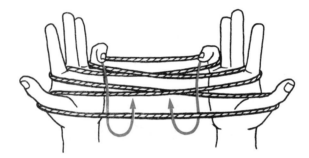

4. Each little finger now has two loops. You want to Navaho these loops. Make sure that the new far little finger string (the one you just picked up from your thumbs), stays above the old far little finger string.

   Your right index finger and thumb pick up the lower far little finger string near your left little finger, carry it over the top of your left little finger, and let it lie in the centre of the figure.

   Your left index finger and thumb pick up the lower far little finger string near your right little finger, carry it over the top of your right little finger, and let it lie in the centre of the figure.

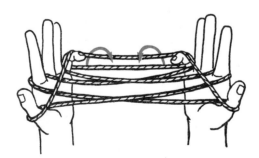

The loops you have just Navahoed must stay on the far side of the index loops.

5. There is a palmar string which crosses each index loop. Hook your index fingers over these strings and down into the index loops.

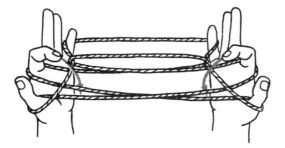

6. Put your foot into the big loop held by your little fingers, and take your little fingers out.

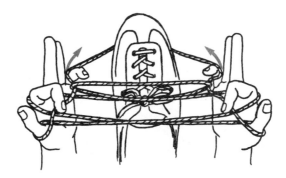

7. Now drop the loops from your thumbs. Each thumb can push off the opposite thumb loop, but hold on tightly to the strings under your index fingers as you do this. The loops on your index fingers will slip off by themselves.

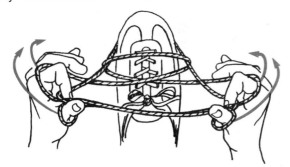

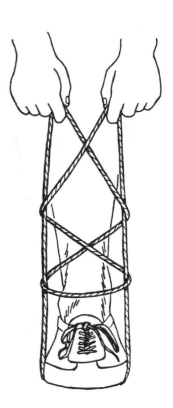

8. Pull gently with your index fingers and you will see the man with his arms and legs wrapped around the tree.

9. To make him climb the tree, pull gently with your right index finger, then with your left. As you keep doing this, he will climb higher and higher.

Flying Parrot

This figure came from British Guiana. You should hold the long hanging loop fairly close to the body of the figure to make a short-tailed "kawack," or green parrot. This bird flies as well.

1. Put the string loop between the index and middle fingers of your left hand. The long part of the loop hangs down across your palm.

2. With your right hand, take hold of the short part of the loop. Bring this string loop forward over your index and middle fingers.

3. Make an X in the loop you are holding by giving it half a twist 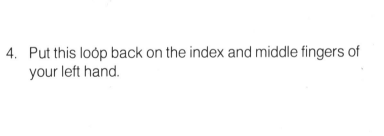 clockwise.

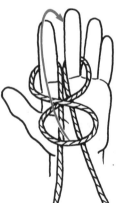

4. Put this loop back on the index and middle fingers of your left hand.

5. Pull down the loops that go around your left index and middle fingers to make these loops a bit bigger.

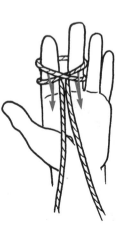

6. Two strings come from between your left index and middle finger. With your right index finger and thumb, pick up the string nearest to your left thumb (string 1) and put it around the back of your left thumb.

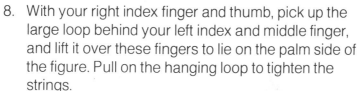

7. With your right index finger and thumb, pick up string 2, the one nearest to your left little finger and put it around the back of your left little finger.

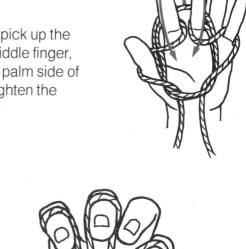

8. With your right index finger and thumb, pick up the large loop behind your left index and middle finger, and lift it over these fingers to lie on the palm side of the figure. Pull on the hanging loop to tighten the strings.

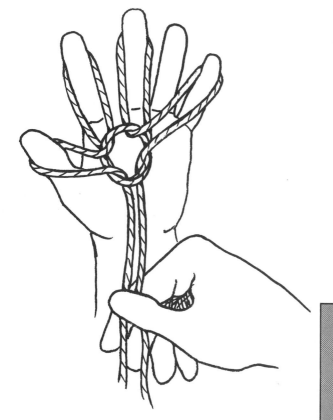

How to make the parrot fly

1. Move all the loops up near the tips of your fingers.
2. Spread your fingers wide and hold the hanging loop lightly.
3. Let your fingers collapse and pull down on the hanging loop.

Lightning

Lightning is another Navaho figure. With a little practice, you can make your string lightning flash into its zigzag pattern—just the way real lightning flashes across the sky.

Lightning begins with the **Navaho opening.**

1. Hold the string loop with your hands about ten centimetres apart.

2. Make a small loop in the string you are holding.

3. Put your index fingers from behind into this string loop. Your index fingers are pointing towards you.

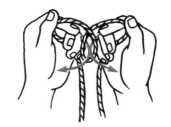

4. Turn your index fingers down, away from you, and up. The rest of your fingers are still holding on to the hanging strings of the big loop.

5. The strings you are holding with your hands cross in the middle to make an X.

   Your thumbs bring forward the bottom strings of the X and pull them out as far as they will go.

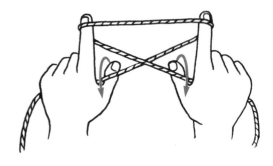

This is the Navaho opening.

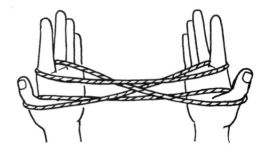

6. Your thumbs go over the near index strings to get the far index strings and return. Now you are going to weave the lightning.

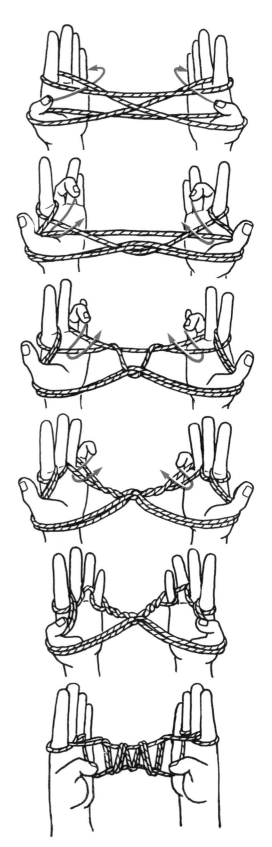

7. Your middle fingers go over the near index strings to get the far thumb strings and return.

8. Your ring fingers go over the far middle finger strings to get the near index strings and return.

9. Your little fingers go over the far ring finger strings to get the far middle finger strings and return.

Press the fingers of each hand tightly together so that the loops at the base of your fingers cannot move. If the strings between your fingers slide, you can't extend the lightning.

10. Move your thumbs across to the far ring finger strings. By pressing down on them with your thumbs, you will untwist the strings you have woven and make the lightning flash across the sky.

The Yam Thief

The Inuit called this string figure the Mouse and squeaked as they pulled the string off the fingers. In South America, it represented a snake crawling in and out of the trees. It also illustrated the tale of some stolen yams.

1. Hang the string loop over the fingers and thumb of your left hand.

2. Put your right hand into the hanging loop so that both hands are facing in the same direction. Use your right index finger like a hook to take hold of the string that crosses the space between your left thumb and index finger.

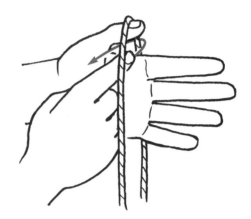

3. Now, with your right index finger, pull out a short loop in this string. Pull the loop out under the string that hangs over your left thumb. You must keep this loop straight.

4. Hold this loop with your right index finger and thumb and give it half a twist clockwise (make an X in it towards your left little finger).

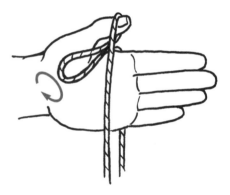

5. Put this loop on your left index finger, and pull on the hanging loop to tighten the strings. Be careful not to twist the loop again when you put it on your finger.

Now you repeat this to put loops on the rest of your fingers. Keep one string hanging down across your palm and one hanging down the back of your hand. Always put your right index finger under the string hanging down across your palm and use it like a hook.

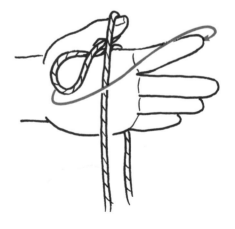

6. Pull out a loop, in the back string, between your index finger and middle finger. Make sure you pull it out under the string that hangs across your palm. Give it half a twist ↻ clockwise and put it on your middle finger. Tighten the strings.

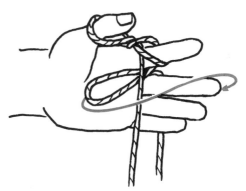

7. Pull out a loop between your middle finger and ring finger, give it a half twist ↻ clockwise, and put it on your ring finger. Tighten the strings.

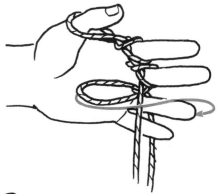

8. Pull out a loop between your ring finger and little finger, give it half a twist ↻ clockwise and put it on your little finger. Tighten the strings.

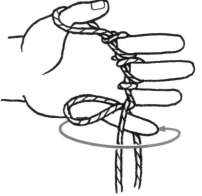

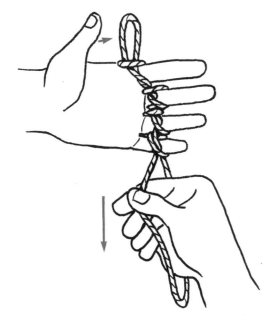

The loops on your fingers are the bags of yams tied up and ready for the thief's quick escape. The thumb loop is the farmer or master of the yam field. When you take the loop off your thumb, the farmer wakes up. Pull the front string of the hanging loop, and the thief escapes with all the yams!

A Bird

This bird comes from Papua in New Guinea. You can make him fly across the string—but only in one direction!

1. Do Position 1 on your left hand.

2. With your right index finger and thumb, pull out the left palmar string as far as it will go.

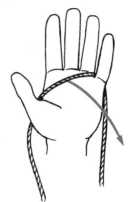

3. With your right index finger and thumb, pull out the new left palmar string as far as it will go.

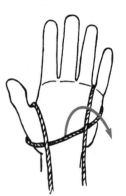

4. Put your right thumb and little finger from the front, into the hanging loop.

5. From the outside, put your right thumb into the left thumb loop and, also from the outside, put your right little finger into the left little finger loop.

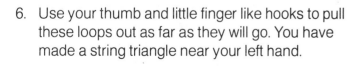

6. Use your thumb and little finger like hooks to pull these loops out as far as they will go. You have made a string triangle near your left hand.

7. Take your right thumb and little finger out of the loops they are holding. From the front, near the string triangle, put your right thumb into the hanging thumb loop, and your right little finger into the hanging little finger loop.

8. Put these fingers up behind the string which makes the base of the string triangle.

9. Gently draw this string out as far as it will go. Now there is a string diamond near your right hand. (If you pull too hard, the diamond, and the bird, will be too small.)

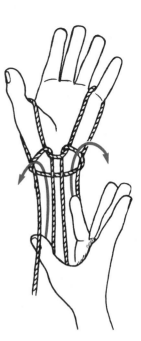

10. There is a loop which runs out from between your left little finger and ring finger, down to the diamond and back between your left index finger and thumb. With your left index finger and thumb, pick up this loop inside the diamond and put it on your right index finger.

   See saw your hands away from each other to tighten the strings a little.

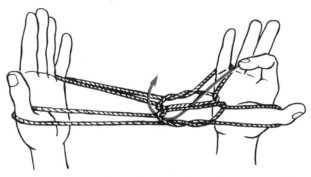

11. Drop the loops from your right thumb and little finger (these loops are the wings), and pull with your right index finger to make the bird fly along the string.

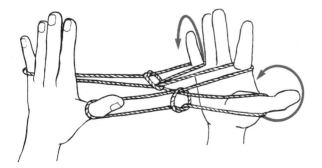
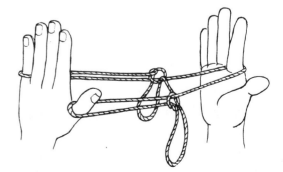

The Fly

This version of the Fly comes from the Solomon Islands which are near New Guinea in the Pacific Ocean. It was also known as a mosquito, a locust, and even a flying fox.

You clap your hands together to try and catch that fly, but when you pull your hands apart, you'll find the fly has escaped again. Maybe your friends will have better luck!

1. Hang the string loop on your little fingers.

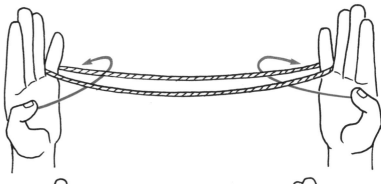

2. Your thumbs get both strings of the little finger loops.

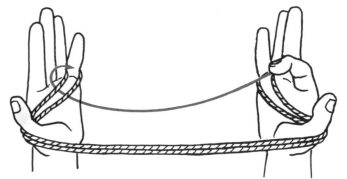

3. Your right index finger gets the two left palmar strings.

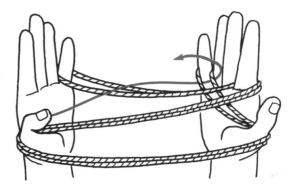

4. Your left thumb goes over the far index strings to pick up from below, the two right palmar strings, not between but beside, the strings of the right index loop.

5. Navaho the left thumb loops.

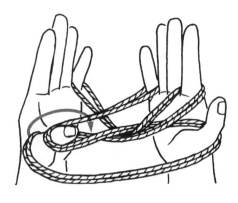

6. Your right thumb drops its loops. Now, pull the strings tight.

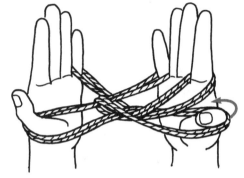

7. Your left thumb and right index finger drop their loops to release the fly's wings. Don't pull with your little fingers yet.

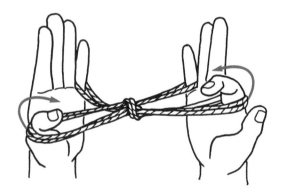

8. You clap your hands to catch the fly.

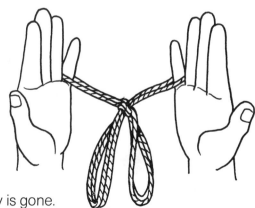

9. Your little fingers now pull out their loops to show that the fly is gone.

Man on a Bed

This figure comes from the Torres Straits. After you have made the Man on a Bed, chant:

> Man on a bed, man on a bed
> Lies asleep, lies asleep,
> The bed breaks.

When the bed breaks, the man falls out!

1. Do Opening A. Keep the index loops near the tips of your index fingers.

2. Your thumbs go under the index loops to get the near little finger strings and return under the strings of the index loops.

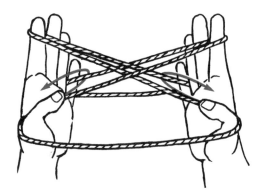

3. Your little fingers hook down the far index strings.

4. Your little fingers get the far thumb strings. They return through the strings of the index loops.

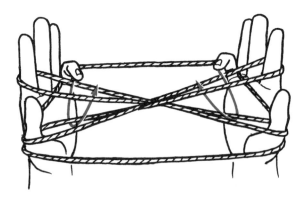

5. Your index fingers drop their loops to make ...

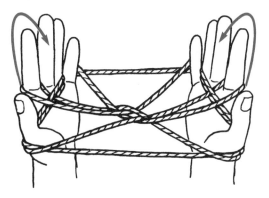

6. ... the Man on a Bed.

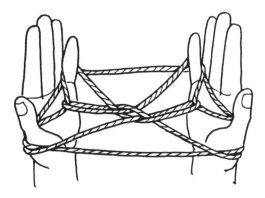

7. To make the bed break, drop both loops from your little fingers and pull with your thumbs.

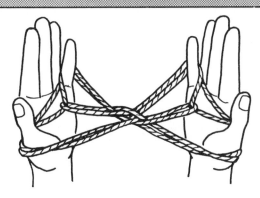

Apache Door

This is a Navaho figure which shows the decorated door flap of an Apache tent. It is longer and more difficult than many of the other figures in this book, but the finished pattern is very beautiful. Don't forget to rub your hands together to summon the magic which will make the figure appear.

1. Do Position 1.

2. Put your whole right hand under the left palmar string and as you pull it out, let the string loop slide down around your right wrist.

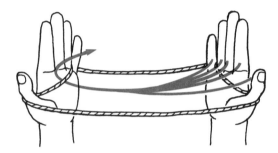

3. Put your whole left hand, thumb too, under the right palmar string and, as you pull it out, let the string loop slide down around your left wrist.

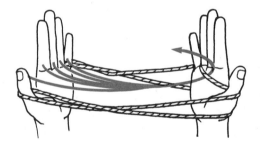

4. Your thumbs get the near little finger strings and return.

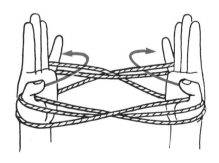

5. Your little fingers get the far thumb strings and return.

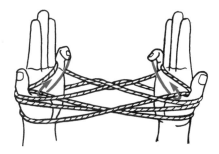

6. With your whole right hand, take hold of all the strings in the middle of the figure.

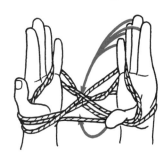

7. Put all these strings between your left index finger and thumb. Make sure these strings don't cover up the thumb loops—you'll need these. Then let go of the strings you are holding with your right hand.

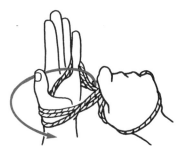

8. Now, use your right index finger and thumb to take hold of the two left thumb loops and hang on to them. Don't move this right hand at all.

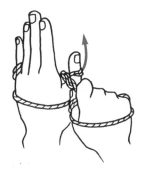 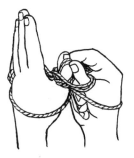

Keep going ...

9. Take your left thumb out of these two thumb loops and out of the strings you have just wrapped around it.

10. From below, slide your left thumb back into the two loops that your right index finger and thumb have been holding.

11. Repeat this for your right hand. So, with your left hand, take hold of all the strings in the middle of the figure.

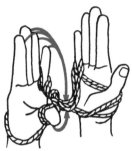

12. Put all these strings between your right index finger and thumb.

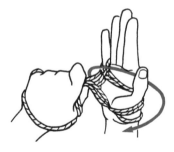

13. With your left index finger and thumb, take hold of the two right thumb loops and hang on to them. Remember not to move your left hand.

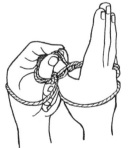

14. Take your right thumb out of these two thumb loops and out of the strings you have just wrapped around it.

15. From below, slide your right thumb back into the loops held by your left index and thumb.

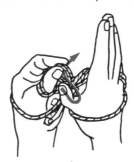

16. With your right index finger and thumb, take the left wrist loop right off your left hand and let it lie in the middle of the figure.

17. With your left index finger and thumb, take the right wrist loop right off your right hand and let it lie in the middle of the figure.

*Now comes the most important part. Put your hands together and rub the strings to summon the magic you will need to make the figure appear.

18. Extend the figure by pulling your hands apart. For best results, see saw your hands up and down a little as you do this.

Cat's Cradle

The game of Cat's Cradle probably travelled from Asia to Europe with the tea trade in the seventeenth century. We know that children in England played Cat's Cradle as early as 1782, because a writer named Charles Lamb talked about weaving "cat-cradles" with his friends when he was at school.

To play this game, you need two people. In most Cat's Cradle figures, you can see X's and straight strings. One person holds the figure while the other picks up the X's and takes them over, under, or between the straight strings. The players take turns holding the figure and picking up the X's to move to the next step.

The game can go on forever, but if you want to stop, you can choose one of several different endings—at various points along the way.

There are many different ways to pick up the X's, so keep playing and keep experimenting. And watch the instructions for clues to the Mystery Figures!

As you play the game, make sure you are holding your strings securely before your partner takes his/her hands out of the figure.

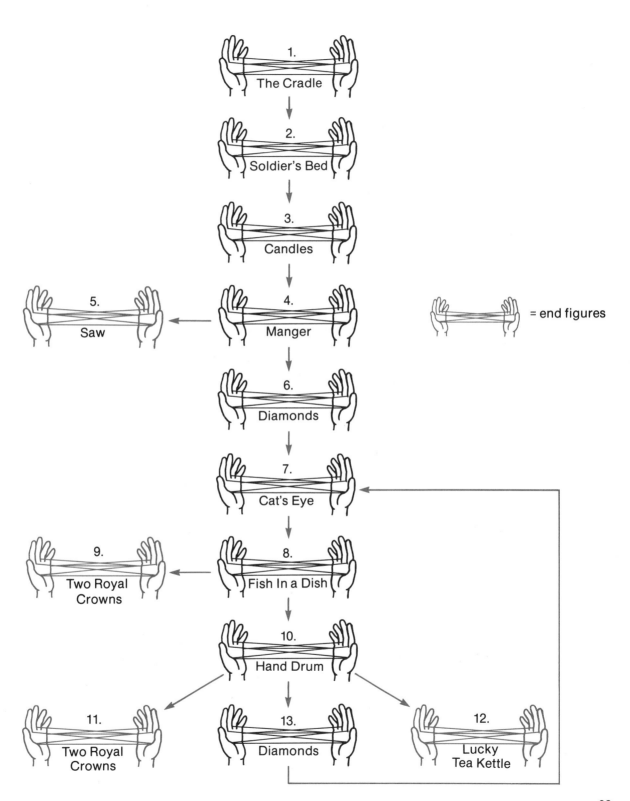

1. The Cradle

2. Soldier's Bed

3. Candles

5. Saw ← 4. Manger

= end figures

6. Diamonds

7. Cat's Eye

9. Two Royal Crowns ← 8. Fish In a Dish

10. Hand Drum

11. Two Royal Crowns

13. Diamonds

12. Lucky Tea Kettle

Cat's Cradle 1: The Cradle

A makes the Cradle

1. Put the string loop around the backs of the fingers (but not the thumb) of each hand.

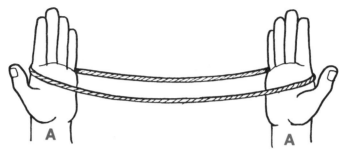

2. Your right index finger and thumb pick up the near string of the loop around your left hand and wrap it once around your left hand. The string comes out between your left index finger and thumb.

3. Your left index finger and thumb pick up the near string of the loop around your right hand and wrap it once around your right hand. Make sure you always pick up the **near** string. One near and one far string wrapped around will give you tangled candles later on.

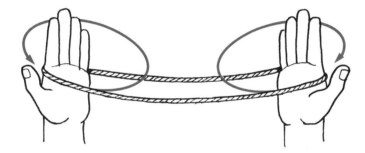

4. Now complete as in Opening A using your middle fingers.

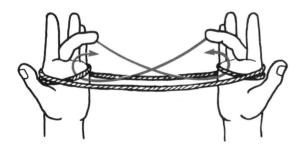
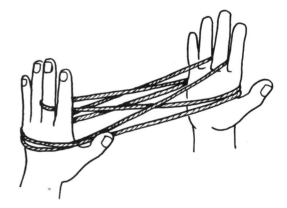

Cat's Cradle 2: The Cradle to Soldier's Bed

B makes the Bed

1. Your index fingers and thumbs take hold of the X's at the sides of the figure.

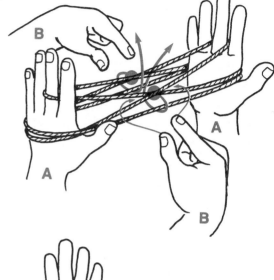

2. Pull the X's out to the sides.

3. Push the X's down and take them under the long side framing strings at the bottom of the figure. Now, turn your index fingers and thumbs up.

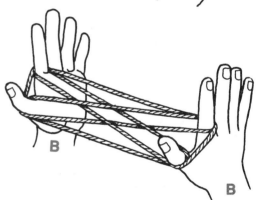

4. Separate your index fingers and thumbs to make the Bed.

In Germany, the game of Cat's Cradle was called Hexenspiel, or Witch's Game. In Japan, Cat's Cradle for two people was called "woof pattern string-taking."

Cat's Cradle 3: Soldier's Bed to Candles

A makes Candles

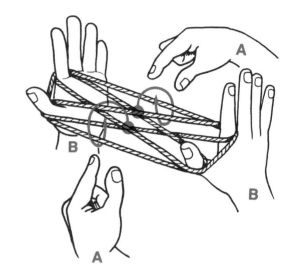

1. Your index fingers and thumbs take the long X's.

2. Pull the X's up, out past the framing strings of the figure.

3. Push the X's down and under the straight framing strings. Now, turn your index fingers and thumbs up.

4. Separate your index fingers and thumbs to make Candles.

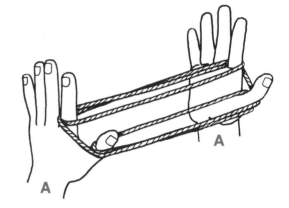

Inuit boys were not allowed to play cat's cradles for fear that when they were hunters, their fingers would become tangled in the harpoon lines.

Cat's Cradle 4: Candles to Manger

B makes the Manger

1. Use your left little finger, face up, like a hook, to get the far thumb candle string and pull it across the figure out past the far index strings. Hang on to this string.

2. Then, use your right little finger, face up, like a hook, to get the near index candle string and pull it across the figure out past the near thumb strings.

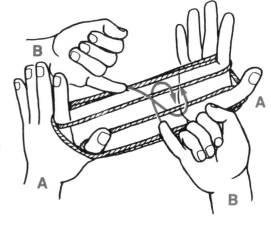

3. Now, your right index finger and thumb go down into the string triangle between the framing strings of the figure and the string held by your right little finger. In the same way, your left index finger and thumb go down into the string triangle held by your left little finger.

4. Your index fingers and thumbs go under, then pick up on their backs, the straight framing strings of the figure.

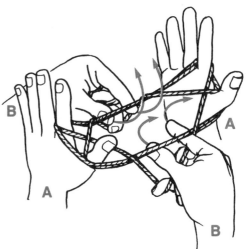

5. Continue to hold the little finger strings securely and separate your index fingers and thumbs to make the Manger.

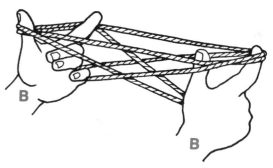

You can end the game here by making the Saw (figure 5). If you want to continue, go on to make Diamonds (figure 6).

Cat's Cradle 5: Manger to Saw

end figure

A makes the Saw and ends the game

1. A takes the top framing side strings of the figure.

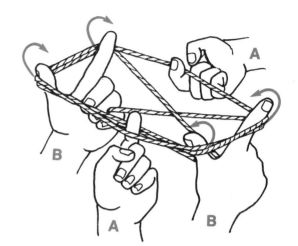

2. B drops the strings from his/her index fingers and thumbs but continues to hold the little finger loops.

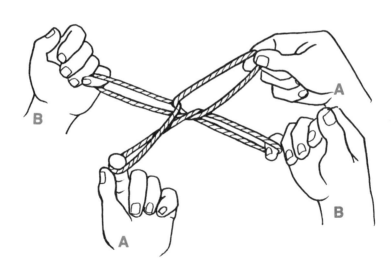

Cat's Cradle 6: Manger to Diamonds

A makes Diamonds

1. Your index fingers and thumbs take the long X's at the sides of the figure.

2. Pull the X's out, then up.

3. Now, take the X's across and over the top framing strings of the figure and point your index fingers and thumbs down into the centre of the figure.

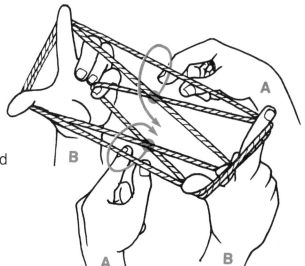

4. Separate your index fingers and thumbs to make Diamonds.

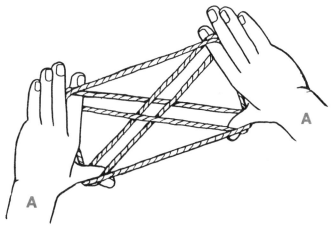

Sometimes, two Maori players would choose a string pattern, then sitting back to back, make it. Afterwards, they would compare the finished figures.

Cat's Cradle 7: Diamonds to Cat's Eye

B Makes Cat's Eye

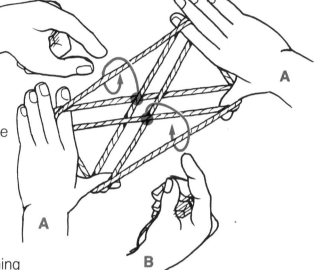

1. Your index fingers and thumbs take the long X's.

2. Pull them up and out past the framing strings of the figure.

3. Now push them down and under the straight framing strings, and turn your index fingers and thumbs up.

4. Separate your index fingers and thumbs to make Cat's Eye.

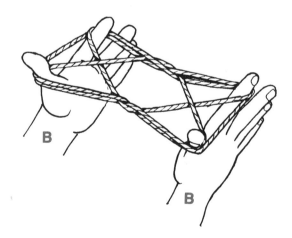

Cat's Cradle 8: Cat's Eye to Fish in a Dish

A makes Fish in a Dish

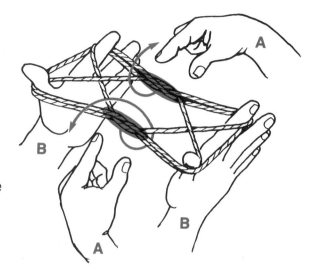

1. Your index fingers and thumbs go down into the loops held by B's index fingers and thumbs, and pinch the sides of the central diamond where they meet the framing strings.

2. Turn your index fingers and thumbs up into the large central diamond of the figure.

3. Separate your index fingers and thumbs to make Fish in a Dish.

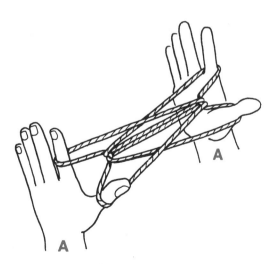

You can end the game here by making Two Royal Crowns (figure 9). If you want to continue, go on to make Hand Drum or Scraggly (figure 10).

Cat's Cradle 9: Fish in a Dish to Two Royal Crowns

B makes Two Royal Crowns and ends the game

1. Your index fingers and thumbs take the long X's and pull them out to the sides to make the Crowns.

   This figure is also called Grandfather Clock.

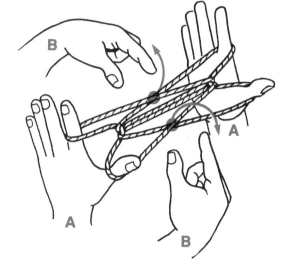

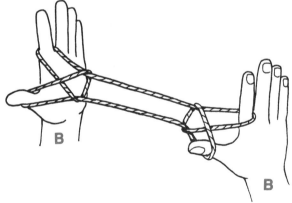

The Inuit also played cat's cradles in the fall to catch the sun in the meshes of their strings and so delay the coming of the long winter night.

Cat's Cradle 10: Fish in a Dish to Hand Drum or Scraggly

B makes the Drum

This time, the X's are on the outside and the straight strings are in the centre.

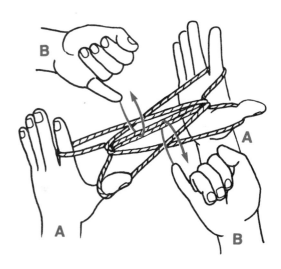

1. Each little finger takes the straight central string nearest to it and pulls it out past the X's. Hang on to these strings. There is now a central diamond framed by the X's.

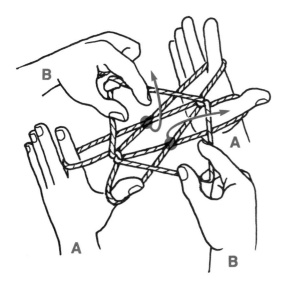

2. Now, your index fingers and thumbs take the X's as usual.

3. Still holding the little finger strings, turn your index fingers and thumbs up into the central diamond.

4. Separate your index fingers and thumbs to complete the Hand Drum.

You can end the game here by making Two Royal Crowns (figure 11) or the Lucky Tea Kettle (figure 12). If you want to continue, go on to make Diamonds (figure 13).

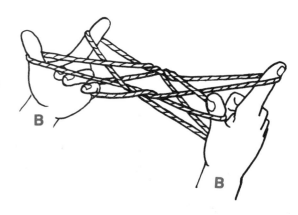

Cat's Cradle 11: Hand Drum to Two Royal Crowns or Grandfather Clock

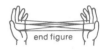
end figure

B makes the Crowns and ends the game

1. Release the loops from your little fingers to make Two Royal Crowns.

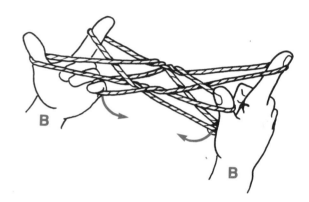

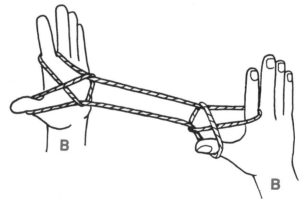

> The Kiwi Papuans used to use cat's cradle strings to tie the new yam shoots to their supporting sticks. Magically, the yam shoots would twine around their sticks the way the strings had twined around their fingers.

Cat's Cradle 12: Hand Drum to the Lucky Tea Kettle

end figure

It takes three people to make the Lucky Tea Kettle. Go and call a friend.

In Japan, they end the game this way. Each person takes two loops of the Hand Drum figure.

1. B is holding the Drum and keeps the loops on his/her index fingers.

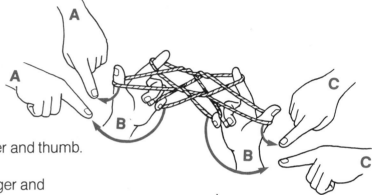

2. A takes the loops from B's left little finger and thumb.

3. C takes the loops from B's right little finger and thumb.

This is the Hibachi on which the Lucky Tea Kettle is put to boil. But, according to the Japanese fairy tale, the Lucky Tea Kettle is no ordinary tea kettle. It is, in fact, a talented badger tea kettle named Bumbuku-Chagama. When the kettle becomes a badger, his head with two bright eyes looks out of the spout, and four brown hairy paws and a bushy tail appear. You can imagine the clatter and clang as the Lucky Tea Kettle, complaining loudly, jumps off the fire!

To end the game, the three people holding the strings of the Hibachi, shout "Chan-garagara!" which is the noise of the tea kettle jumping off the fire. Then they all let go of their strings at once. The one left holding the strings loses the game.

Cat's Cradle 13: Hand Drum to Diamonds

A makes Diamonds

First, you have to find the X's. The strings that make the X's run up from B's little fingers. The figure has two lower loops held by B's little fingers, and four upper loops held by B's index fingers and thumbs.

1. Put your index fingers and thumbs from each side of the figure into the space between the upper and lower loops. Your index fingers and thumbs are touching the strings of both little finger loops. Slide your index fingers and thumbs towards each other along the strings of the little finger loops until they close on the strings that lace together in the middle of each side of the figure.

   When you pull these strings out to the sides, the X's should come free, leaving only two straight framing strings.

2. Your index fingers and thumbs pull the X's out to the sides.

3. Now, take the X's towards each other over the framing strings.

4. Turn your index fingers and thumbs down into the centre space of the figure.

5. Separate your index fingers and thumbs to make Diamonds.

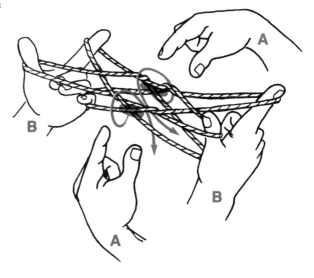

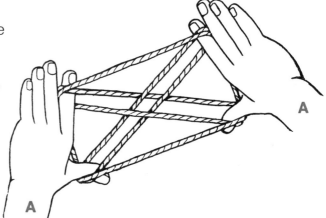

Cat's Cradle: Mystery Figures

Now that you have played Cat's Cradle to the end, you are ready to experiment with some mystery figures. These are variations of the moves you made the first time around, but you will see that the results are quite different.

Cat's Eye Mystery Figure

This figure is a bit tricky, so you'll probably have to look at the pictures.

First, follow the instructions from the beginning of the Cradle (figure 1), to the end of figure 7, Cat's Eye.

Now, your little fingers pull out the strings that make the sides of the central diamond, just where they lace through the side framing strings.

What happens when your index fingers and thumbs turn down and under the framing strings, then up into the centre of the figure?

Fish in a Dish Mystery Figures

There are two possible variations.

1. First, follow the instructions from the Cradle (figure 1), to the end of figure 8, Fish in a Dish.

    Now, see what happens when you take the long X's down into the centre of the figure between the two central straight strings.

2. To do the second Fish in a Dish Mystery Figure, again follow the instructions to the end of Figure 8.

    What figure do you get when you take the X's up into the centre of the figure from below, between the two straight central strings?

Hand Drum Mystery Figure

First, follow the instructions from the Cradle (figure 1), to the end of figure 10. When you have the Hand Drum, you will need to find the X's as you did at the beginning of figure 13. If you've forgotten where they are, read instruction 1 for figure 13 again.

Now, see what happens when you take the X's down under the framing strings and up into the centre of the figure.

The spirit of cat's cradles came to Inuit children who played at string figures late at night. The spirit made a strange sound like the crackling of dry skins and challenged the maker of string figures to a race, to see who could make Opening A faster. If the child or other member of his family won, the spirit would vanish and the family would be saved.

ABOUT THE AUTHOR

CAMILLA GRYSKI always carries string in her pocket. Formerly a children's librarian for the Toronto Public Library system, she now works as a librarian at the Hospital for Sick Children. Ms. Gryski has demonstrated string figures at schools and libraries across Ontario and at folk festivals across Canada.